SPORT
OF
CROSS COUNTRY SKI-ING

The
SPUR BOOK
of
CROSS COUNTRY SKI-ING

by
Terry Brown and Rob Hunter

SPURBOOKS LIMITED

Published by
SPURBOOKS LIMITED
6 Parade Court
Bourne End
Buckinghamshire

The authors would like to thank Randy Hooper of A.B.C. Sports, Vancouver B.C. Canada, the staff of the Y.H.A. Ski-shop, London and Rene Brivadis, President of the Foyer du Sku-de-Fond, La Chaise-Dieu, Auvergne, France, for their help in preparing this book.

ISBN 0 904978 85 0

Printed by Maund & Irvine, Ltd., Tring, Herts.

CONTENTS

INTRODUCTION

ABOUT THIS SERIES
Venture Guides fall into two broad categories. The first aims to provide a range of essential information on a range of outdoor skills, and covers such subjects as Knot Tying and Splicing, Map and Compass Work, First Aid, Weather Lore, Camping Skills, and Survival and Rescue Techniques.

The second category relates to what we describe as Venture Sports, which are not team games, or activities requiring mechanical assistance, but include such subjects as Sailing, Snorkelling, Rock Climbing, Backpacking, Hill Trekking, Ski-ing, and now, the subject of this book, Cross Country Ski-ing.

ABOUT THIS BOOK
Throughout the world, outdoor activities in general, and Cross Country Ski-ing in particular, is enjoying an unprecedented boom.

Langláuf; Nordic; Ski-wandering; XC; Ski-de-fond. A wide range of names for the same thing, all indicating the worldwide popularity of XC, from Australia to Alaska, not only in traditional Nordic areas, but also in the resorts and retreats formerly the preserve of the downhill Alpine ski-er, who, until very recently had scarcely seen the lightly-equipped, slender ski-ed devotees of the oldest form of ski-ing we know.

This book will introduce the non-skier and the Alpine skier, to the basics of Cross Country Ski-ing. It will describe the terrain, the equipment, the clothing, the techniques and the technicalities.

As happens with many sports, cross country ski-ing is subdivided into several areas; ski-touring and ski-mountaineering, to name but two. Detailed books on these aspects of the sport will follow, but this one just aims to get you started, trained and equipped—a basic introduction to a new and fascinating activity.

Chapter 1

WHAT IS CROSS COUNTRY SKI-ING?

Historically, cross-country ski-ing is the original form of the sport, dating back probably to prehistoric times.

Certainly there are cave paintings from the Neolithic period, around 30,000BC which appear to show people on skis. Alpine ski-ing, on the other hand, is barely a hundred years old, although in that time it has come to dominate the sport, and even oust cross-country or Nordic ski-ing from dominance in its traditional areas.

Perhaps before we go any further, we had better clear up the problem of the name. Cross-country ski-ing, as we have noted, has a variety of names, with practically every country, and certainly every language having its own. We use the term 'cross country ski-ing' as the name for the sport in this book because it is the most descriptive, both of the sport itself, and of those areas we will cover in this book. We will refer to it as 'ski-ing' and refer to Alpine ski-ing as "downhill" ski-ing.

A DEFINITION

Cross country ski-touring is the process of moving on skis, over snow-covered terrain, off the downhill 'piste', either through deep untrodden snow, or on prepared cross-country tracks. It employs equipment which differs in many ways from downhill equipment which is used on different terrain, and requires a number of different and supporting skills.

Exactly what these skills and differences are we shall cover in subsequent chapters.

WHY CROSS COUNTRY?

It is reasonable to enquire into this current renaissance of cross country ski-ing, for it is booming away in many countries, but the reasons are not hard to seek.

First of all, given snow cover of a few inches, you can XC-ski anywhere, so that it opens up vast areas unsuited to the downhill ski-er.

COST

Secondly, compared with downhill, cross-country is cheap. A complete and adequate set of skis, boots, poles and bindings, can be bought for about £50, less than $100 U.S. dollars, although you can pay much more if you want to. You don't need lifts, which, with Alpine lift passes reaching about £25 (say $50) a week is a great saving, and you can avoid the crowds on the slopes and congestion on the lifts.

CLOTHING

While you *can* buy attractive and colourful XC garments, you can get along very well in just warm and comfortable old clothes, which is another saving. (Fig. 2)

IS IT DULL?

No, it isn't.

If you have been a downhill ski-er, with the occasional lift-borne tour thrown in, you will probably find, when you try cross-country, that this is the sort of ski-ing you wanted when you took up the sport. On cross-country skis you can get away from the crowds, and get that exhilaration and sense of freedom that can no longer be found on crowded 'pistes'.

XC requires a good standard of ski-ing and while you usually climb up, there is always the downhill swoop to follow, through the deep, unmarked snow, to give you a thrill and test your skills.

AGE

Age is no barrier to cross-country. You can start very young, and go on for ever. It is less dangerous to limbs than downhill, and gives more physical satisfaction. Given a steady start, and good technique you will not find it too exhausting. You don't need to be super-fit, (although it helps) but cross-country will get and keep you fit. Cross-country will appeal to those who like the outdoors for itself, to walkers, hikers, campers and ramblers — as well as ski-ers. If you want to get about in the winter, do it on cross-country skis.

WHERE CAN YOU GO XC?

Almost anywhere, is the short answer. All you need is snow, Traditionally, cross-country has been firmly based in the Scandinavian countries, Norway, Sweden, Finland, and it still is. Their equipment and techniques set the standard for the world. But the sport has spread widely. Canada and the U.S.A. have huge cross-country areas, Australia and New Zealand are experiencing a boom, while in France the Pyrenees, the Auvergne, and the Vosges, all specialize in cross-country, and XC is now seen, a little more each year, in the committed Alpine ski resorts.

It is still difficult, outside Scandinavia and North America, to find holidays devoted to cross-country ski-ing, but this will undoubtedly come. Meanwhile, it certainly exists at more and more downhill resorts, and you can sample it under private arrangements when you get there.

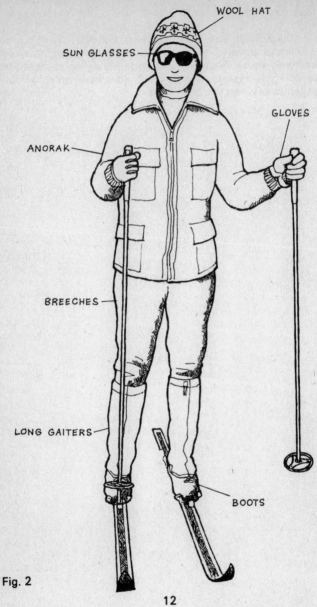

WOOL HAT

SUN GLASSES

GLOVES

ANORAK

BREECHES

LONG GAITERS

BOOTS

Fig. 2

12

Chapter 2

CLOTHING

It is fair to say that, initially anyway, any old sports clothes will do. However, a wide range of attractive and suitable gear exists, at reasonable prices, and it may be comforting to look the part even if, to begin with, you can't manage the technique. (Fig. 2)

BODY HEAT AND VENTILATION

Even though you are out in the snow, at below or near zero temperatures, you will not be cold if you keep moving. The exercise will keep you warm, but it is important to keep as cool and as free from perspiration as possible. If your clothing gets damp from sweat, it loses most of the insulation properties, and you will chill rapidly when you stop unless you then put on windproof garments to keep the wind out until your body cools.

Bear in mind that the real chill comes from cooling perspiration, not from the effect of the cold air. Your garments, therefore, must be lightweight and of a natural material, equipped with buttons or zips to aid ventilation while moving, but enabling you to cover up quickly and retain warmth when you stop.

Cross-country ski-ing is warm work, so for a normal day's outing the clothes tend to be lightweight, and must allow free movement.

Leaving aside the boots, which will be covered in the next chapter, let us start at the feet and work up.

STOCKINGS

You need to wear two pairs. One long pair, knee-length, and preferably of oiled wool, and a short pair, of just over ankle length, to go on top of the first long pair. The idea is that you fold the top of the short pair over the boot, to make a better seal against the snow. Personally, I think gaiters do a neater and better job, so I wear gaiters as well.

BREECHES

Breeches, (or knickers, as they call them in North America) are the ideal lower garment for the cross-country ski-er. I have a pair of lightweight breeches in a tough tweed-mix. They fasten, below the knee, over the stockings, with Velcro strips, have button through pockets and a double seat. I use them for hill walking and scrambling in the summer, and for cross-country work in winter. Ordinary outdoor trousers or stretch ski-pants can be temporarily transformed into breeches by simply rolling long stockings up over them to the knee.

SWEATSHIRTS

A light T-shirt, not too tight under the arms, is ideal. Any old wool or cotton shirt will do. This soaks up the sweat, and retains some insulation properties when you stop.

ANORAK/PARKA

Over the top goes a light single-skin anorak in proofed nylon. It has a full length zip, as it is usually open when on the move. Zipped and flapped pockets keep the wet out and the flaps prevent the zips from freezing. It is a good idea to have a hood, which can be rolled back into the collar, until needed.

HAT

Many cross-country ski-ers favour a peaked hat, which keeps twigs out of your eyes when dodging under trees.

One of these, or a wool hat which can be pulled over the ears is fine. I also carry an ear-band, which is very handy in the warm days. Hats soak up sweat from the head and forehead, and when ski-ers stop for a snack or chat it's not unusual to see the sweat freezing up on their hat bands!

GLOVES

Gloves get pretty wet, so a good pair which retain their insulation when damp via an absorbent lining is a worthwhile buy. Strong leather palms and fingers, matched with a breathable meshed top would be fine. Buy a pair big enough to get a cotton pair on as well, to keep you warm in bad weather. Some folk swear by mittens, but since they are always having to come off —to open the pack or fiddle with the compass, I prefer gloves.

SKI-SUITS

As cross-country ski-ing grows in popularity, a whole wardrobe of lightweight, attractive clothing is coming on to the market. They are usually made of light cotton, or breathable nylon, in striking colours, and are very glamorous. They are available in two-part outfits, or as a complete overall.

UNDERWEAR

Unless it is very cold, excessive underwear will simply lead to overheating. A light cotton singlet and pants would probably be best.

SPARE CLOTHING

The above selection will look after you adequately on the move, but it is as well to have some extras, and something to carry them in.

GAITERS

If you wear knee-length gaiters you will have gone a long way towards keeping snow out of your boots, and preventing it from chilling your feet. Even when travelling on prepared tracks, a pair of ankle gaiters or "Stop-Tous" are useful. Long gaiters also come in handy at lunch time, for you can sit on one, insulating the rear, and spread out your lunch on the other. Buy a pair of gaiters as a *basic* item.

SPARE SWEATER/DUVET

A thick wool sweater or a 'duvet' or fibre pile jacket is a useful item for when you stop. Neither need weigh very much, and if rolled up small and tucked into the bottom of the rucksack, they are out of the way and yet to hand if you need them.

SPARE SOCKS

These are always useful. Why be miserable if you can avoid it? In very cold conditions wet feet can be dangerous, so while I would not advise you, in normal conditions, to change the socks the minute you step in a stream (for you might shortly step in another one), if your feet are wet and getting chilled, then change your socks.

SUN GLASSES — GOGGLES

Always have a pair of each.

There is a whole list of bits and pieces, waxes etc., which we shall look at later (see chapter 4) but for them, as for the clothes, you need a rucksack.

Fig. 3

16

Chapter 3

BOOTS, BINDINGS, POLES, SKIS

Cross-country equipment is light. The work it does is hard. It follows therefore, that the equipment must be strong and designed by experts for the job it has to do. It is now much more sophisticated than it was even five years ago, and no doubt variety and innovations will continue to appear.

Do not skimp on equipment, but buy the best you can afford. Fortunately cross-country gear is relatively cheap and if you look after it, it will last for years. Now let's go through the equipment item by item, noting the points to look out for when buying.

BOOTS

At present, and for the foreseeable future, the best boots come from Norway. Insist on Norwegian or at least Scandinavian boots, and you will be on the right track. Above all, the boots *must* fit well. Most boots are now produced to the *Nordic Norm,* which ensures that any boot will fit any binding. (Fig. 3)

When going to buy boots, take with you, or borrow from the shop, the normal two pairs of socks, one thick long pair, and a short, thinner pair.

A cross-country boot looks rather like a running shoe, but if you examine it carefully it has, or should have, some special features. Different types of ski-touring, racing, or mountaineering require different types of boots. Let's look here at touring boots.

The sole at the toe projects into a wide extended flap. On the underside at this point, three holes are drilled into the sole. These are to take the pins on the binding, and it is better if each hole is fitted with a brass sleeve, which stops the holes from becoming ragged or filling in with grit.

Flex the sole. The heel should bend up with supple ease but there should be no sideways movement. Try and twist the instep. It should be impossible, for the instep should be reinforced with a steel or wood insert, to give rigidity against any lateral play. Without this your foot will slip off the ski in the turns.

The boot is single-skinned, usually lined with fur, light and (thank goodness) comfortable. There should be no question of 'breaking in' a cross-country boot — if it isn't comfortable in the shop, try another pair. The types illustrated (Fig. 3) are right for normal cross-country and touring. Heavier boots are needed for ski-mountaineering.

Notice that the boot is single skinned. It will let in the wet, and for this reason you need two pairs of socks, and you should also treat the boot with some water-repellent preparation. The snag is that if it is truly water repellent, it prevents the foot from breathing, and perspiration gets the foot wet anyway. A sensible compromise is to keep the boots clean and well polished, which will help make them waterproof, or use Kiwi wet-prufe.

BINDINGS

As with boots, the choice of binding depends on the type of XC ski-ing you want. For general or light touring the most common and successful binding currently in use is the three-pin Nordic type by Rotefella or Troll. In these, three metal pins in the front of the binding fit into the holes in the boot sole. The binding clamp is then forced down over a spring ratchet, and the toe is clamped securely to the ski. These are also produced to the "Nordic Norm" in standard widths of 71 mm. 75 mm. and 79 mm. The 75 mm. is the most popular. (Fig. 4)

Although the heel can rise, there is also a serrated metal or plastic 'popper' or heel plate, which is situated on the ski, directly under the heel. This will grip the boot heel when your weight is down, for turning or stopping.

Most bindings are a standard 75 mm. size, which will fit most boots. If your feet are very large or very small, you may need to order a special binding. Note that there is a left and right binding and they are usually so marked.

CABLES

Many downhill ski-ers taking up XC, worry about the lack of a cable or clamp securing the boot heel down, when descending, turning or stopping. Given the right technique, practice, and a heel plate, a clamp cable is not necessary and, if fitted to a Nordic binding, positively dangerous. The cable will force the boot into the binding and should you fall, the binding will not release, as a downhill safety binding (usually) does. A broken ski or ankle is the possible outcome. Cable bindings are used by ski-mountaineers where the binding can be adjusted up for climbing, and yet still clamp the heel down for descent. A 'release' safety feature is essential.

There *are* safety bindings for ski-mountaineering, but for normal cross country work they are not necessary, although in some countries cables are a standard fitting.

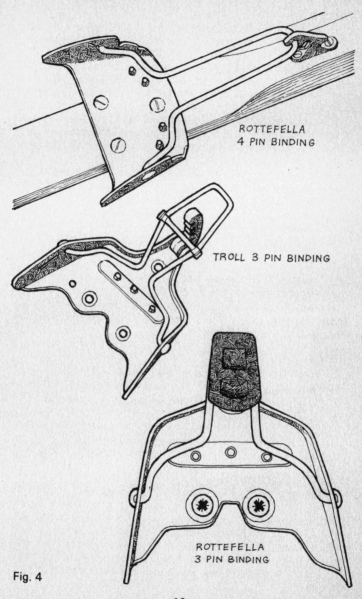

ROTTEFELLA
4 PIN BINDING

TROLL 3 PIN BINDING

ROTTEFELLA
3 PIN BINDING

Fig. 4

19

POLES

Until quite recently all cross-country poles were of Tonkin bamboo. Bamboo poles are still available, inexpensive and very popular. However, having nearly impaled myself when a bamboo pole splintered under me, I have purchased, at moderate cost, an aluminium pair, and I recommend you to do likewise. Fibreglass poles are coming on to the market and they are said to be excellent.

Cross-country poles are long. To be the right length they should fit comfortably into the armpit, like crutches. They would be light in weight, yet strong enough to support your weight while you cross a fence or obstacle.

The straps should be adjustable, and worn under the palms and over the back of the wrist. Note the drawing of the basket and ferrule (Fig. 5). The ferrule tip is slanted forward to ease its exit from the snow as you glide through. The baskets are usually of plastic, and fairly large for greater support off the track or in deep snow. The holes are wide to let the snow slip off easily.

SKIS

Even more than with the downhill variety, you could have a whole book on cross-country skis alone. (Fig. 5)

We have already defined the sort of ski-ing we intend to do, which narrows the choice somewhat. The next decision has more crucial long term effects.

WHICH TYPE OF SKI?

It depends (again) on the type of ski-ing you want. Decide:—
1. If you enjoy backpacking and winter camping.
2. Do you prefer prepared trails, or off-piste deep snow?
3. Do you want to race or tour?
4. Which sort of terrain will you commonly ski over? Downland, hills, woods, fells, mountains?
5. What is your standard of fitness and XC skill?

WAX OR NON-WAX

Until recently, all cross-country skis were made of wood, and all wood needs waxing. Then along came synthetic skis, in came fibreglass, plastic, or polyethylene, which still need waxing but with less preparation. Now there are skis with so-called non-wax surfaces, and, if you buy these your waxing problems are considerably reduced. BUT . . . and there is always a *'but'*, it is undisputed (at present) that waxed skis perform better than the non-waxed.

20

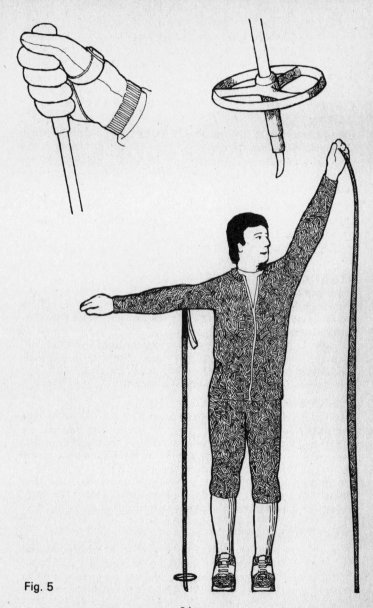

Fig. 5

21

It is therefore likely that if you start cross-country ski-ing and like it you will want to do better, which means waxing. And then what do you do with your step-cut non-wax skis? Let us lay out the broad pros and cons for each type and you can decide for yourself.

There are basically three sorts of cross country ski-ing, and three sorts of skis, differentiated by weight and width.

RACING SKIS

These are very light, around 3 lbs (1.5 kilos), the pair, and made of fibreglass. They are narrow, less than 50 mm (2") wide at the binding, and naturally quite fragile. They are too delicate for general cross-country work, and until you start racing or want to go in for high speed travel, they are not for you.

LIGHT TOURING SKIS

These vary between 52 and 56 mm in width at the binding, and weigh around 4-5 lbs (3 kilos) the pair, and are the best ski for the good ski-er, especially if the bulk of the ski-ing is on prepared trails.

GENERAL TOURING SKIS

If you want to concentrate on climbing hills, or bashing through the woods off prepared trails, then these are the skis for you. They are fairly wide, 56-60 mm (2.25"). As they are wider they give better support in really deep soft snow, and as they are heavier and stiffer some beginners find them easier to manage. However, once you have picked up the technique, they can feel a little cumbersome, weighing anything from 5 to 7 lbs. (3 kilos) the pair, and you may then prefer the light-touring ski.

WHICH SORT OF SKI-ING?

As you can see, the choice of equipment is governed by the type of cross-country ski-ing you have in mind. In this book we are assuming that one starts the sport by touring on tracks or across moderate country. For this the light touring ski is the best but the general touring ski is easier for the beginner. We shall concentrate on describing the general type in this book, and ignore the heavier steel edged ski-mountaineering ski completely—it will feature in our ski-touring book (coming 1978).

SKI-ING SURFACES

The cross-country ski market is in a state of expansion and continual change. New techniques and materials are being introduced all the time. In every case the trend is towards finding a way to avoid waxing, or at least reduce it to running waxes. Let me briefly explain that there are, **basically** two sorts of waxes. "Running" waxes give you grip while you 'kick', yet permit you to slide. **"Base"** waxes hold the running wax to the ski, or base preparation necessary with wooden skis. Running waxes go in the middle of the ski and 'gliding' waxes, a variation, if used at all, go at the end(s). We will cover all this in more detail later.

Please bear with us throughout, on the thorny subject of names. The same items are called different things by different authorities, and vary from country to country.

We try here to **either** define any name or reference, **or** use the most self-explanatory phrase.

SKI TYPES

Broadly speaking, skis come in four basic materials:

1. *Wood:* the best wood skis are made from birch, or hickory, are usually laminated, and edged with lignostone, a hardwood formed from compressed beech. With a wooden ski, the full wax treatment is required, which consists of tarring, preparing with base waxes, then waxing, corking down the running waxes etc. Treated wood holds wax well, and the skis look very beautiful. I fancy, though, that they will slowly disappear or become very costly. It is, of course, possible to get a wood ski with a plastic or fibreglass bottom.

2. *Synthetic Surfaces:* More and more fibreglass, or plastic-soled skis are being produced. They are hard-wearing, and although they don't take wax as well as wood, they need much less preparation. This is particularly true of those fibreglass skis with a plastic bottom. Some models have a numbered waxing scale on the ski sole which lets you know or judge just how large an area you have waxed, which is a useful feature. These need base waxes and running waxes.

3. *Non-wax Step-cut:* The non-wax ski is the latest development. Many such skis now have indentations cut in the sole making a step or fishscale pattern, stretching for about a metre under the foot. The idea is that these patterns grip the snow when you are 'kicking' and yet permit a smooth 'glide' when you move. The makers claim they grip well and need no waxing, which, up to a point, is true. They work very well in 'Klister' conditions (Page 32) but are less effective in powder snow or on ice, make a considerable noise, and in my opinion, need some paraffin glide wax to reduce drag. The pattern can wear out after a while.

4. *Mohair Strips:* This is a variation on the step-cut idea, and is designed to eliminate the need for 'kicking' waxes. Thin mohair strips are let into the base of the ski and they do provide a good grip. They wear well and are easily replaced. I find they are a little less effective in providing a clean glide, but they work very well in temperatures 10°F either side of freezing. They are *very* good in "Klister" conditions. No doubt new types of ski will soon appear.

HOW MUCH SKI-ING

To decide which sort to buy you have to guess how much ski-ing you are going to do. It is safe to suggest fibreglass over wood, but then it depends how much opportunity you are going to get to actually ski, although remember that, providing you've got the snow, you can cross-country ski almost anywhere — the local park, along a footpath, even round the garden. However, if you are an occasional weekend or holiday ski-er, then I would recommend a mohair or step-cut non-wax ski. Waxing is a technique where the ability grows with experience. If you only ski occasionally you will learn little and forget a lot, so a non-wax ski might be less trouble. However, you should still learn about waxes, for even step-cut skis work better with it.

FITTING SKIS

Let us now consider the features you should look for when buying or hiring skis.

LENGTH

Cross-country skis are long. The best guide is to hold the hand up over your head, and choose the ski where the tip fits comfortably into the palm of the upheld hand. Beginners hiring skis might prefer skis a little shorter, say with the tip reaching just to the upheld wrist, while if you are tall or heavy, then perhaps one a little longer would be better. (Fig. 5)

CAMBER AND FLEXIBILITY

Cross-country skis, held base to base, exhibit a considerable curve or "camber". Grasp the skis between fingers and thumb in the high arch, and squeeze them together. Check that they lie flat together all along their length, as any failure to do so indicates distortion.

Camber is the amount of arc or curve in the skis. The amount of resistance to flattening is called 'flex'. Your weight must be spread evenly along the entire length, and it is the 'camber' that does this, and thereby assists the 'kick' and 'glide' phases.

The skis should come together firmly, but without undue difficulty. If they snap together the skis are too soft, too flexible,

Fig. 6

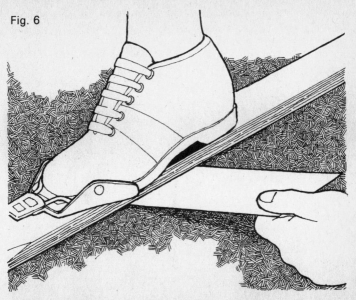

and the tips and tails may rise when your weight goes on them. If they are virtually impossible to squeeze together, they are too stiff, and you may not rest evenly on the snow. So you want skis that you can squeeze together with some little effort.

Try another test. Lay the skis down on a hard even floor (not a carpet) and stand on them. Have the assistant try to slip a piece of paper under them, at the point below your feet. The sheet of paper should slide under easily. If it won't, the skis are too soft for your weight. If, on the other hand you can get a wedge of cardboard under, they are too stiff. (Fig. 6)

Don't neglect these tests.

Let us now summarise. Remember that you do not have to buy, for you can usually hire, even in downhill resorts nowadays and in the beginning, until you are certain that you like cross-country ski-ing, and have decided what sort, and how much you will be able to do, hiring is far the best.

If you buy, we recommend general touring equipment throughout, with fibreglass skis, rather than wood, and that you give serious consideration to a non-wax type, while remembering that they are relatively untried, and less effective. Think it over, talk to the sales assistant, and while you are at it, invest in a few bits and pieces.

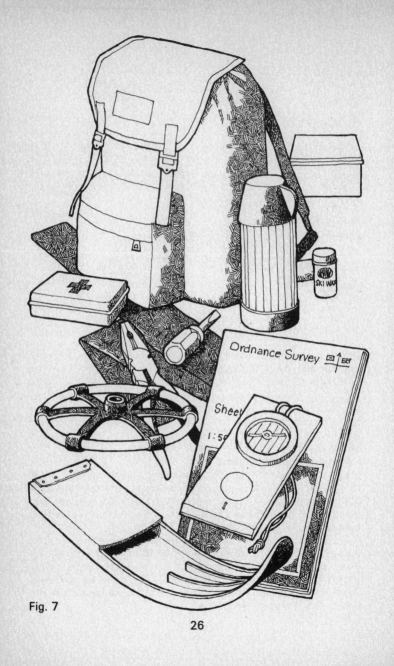

Fig. 7

Chapter 4

ACCESSORIES

For ski-touring, you need a few items which, if you are a summer hiker or camper, you may well possess anyway. (Fig. 7)

TOURING RUCKSACK

A small, light, frameless, nylon rucksack is a useful buy. Karrimor have an excellent selection, and the sort suitable for day hiking is also very suitable for cross-country ski-ing. Try it on and be sure that it fits snugly to the back. Any swaying about will upset your balance while ski-ing. For the same reason a waist belt is useful. Some people use a downhill ski-ers bumbag, but I don't believe these are adequate for cross-country work.

Here are a few items to put in it.

SPARE SKI TIP

This is a hollow replica, in metal or plastic, of a ski tip. It is not difficult to break a ski in the woods and if it shears off when you are in the wilds you'll have trouble getting home. The spare tip fits on to the body of the ski, is secured there with screws or a serrated clamp, and will get you home.

COMPASS

Even on a short outing take a compass, and work out beforehand the bearings to the road or car park. A route card for your day tour is a sensible preparation.

MAP

You need a local map(s) of a scale not less than 1:50,000, and given that winter landmarks are frequently obscured, 1:25000 might be better. Neither map nor compass will help you if you can't use them and if you are unfamiliar with map and compass may we recommend our book, **The Spur Book of Map & Compass,** also published in this series, at 90p.

FIRST AID KIT

A small kit containing bandages, a few plasters, 'Moleskin' for blisters, and some face and sun cream for chapped face and lips, should be carried.

POLE BASKET

It's quite easy also to wrench the basket off the pole, having caught it under some tree root. Ski-ing without a basket is a lopsided affair, so buy a spare, complete with split-pin, and put it in the sack. A plastic or bamboo one weighs next to nothing, and is easily stowed.

SKI-BAG

When you buy your skis buy a bag to carry them in. This is particularly important if you intend transporting the skis by car, in a ski or roof rack. Rain, spray and flying grit harm the skis, and wax won't stick to wet or dirty surfaces. So buy a ski bag.

REPAIR OUTFIT

A small screwdriver and a pair of needle-point pliers are useful.

VACUUM FLASK — FOOD PACK

A meal out, even a picnic lunch, is a great part of the day, and in winter a warm drink is welcome. Prepare it beforehand and take it in a vacuum flask, padding the flask with your extra sweater. Consider taking cold drinks as well. Cross-country ski-ing is thirsty work and you can get dehydrated.

LUNCH BOX

A plastic lunch box, or a Tupperware container is ideal, and weighs very little.

Finally, you will need a wax kit, containing a range of waxes, suitable for your area, and so, let us now look at waxes and waxing.

Chapter 5

WAXES AND WAXING

Nothing so preoccupies the cross country ski-er as waxes and waxing. The subject offers endless opportunities for discussion, argument, expertise and error. To the experienced ski-er all this is great fun, but to the beginner it is confusing and a little worrying. Let us start by assuring the beginner that there is very little to worry about. A few simple rules and guidelines will quickly overcome most of the problems you may encounter.

How much time you spend waxing depends on your skis, which fall into three main types.

1. *Wooden skis:* Wooden skis need the full waxing treatment. The raw wood base must be sealed with tar against wet. This is followed by a base wax, which serves as a 'base' for the full range of running waxes. Tars can be melted on , painted on or come in spray-cans.

2. *Skis with synthetic running surfaces:* Most racing skis, even wooden ones now have synthetic bottoms, of glass or carbon fibre. These need base waxes *and* running waxes.

3. *Non-Wax Skis:* No waxing required; but I have a step-cut pair, and while they are fine for climbing and very effective on the flat, I find them slow downhill, and use a little glide wax on tips and tails.

Waxes come in two basic categories: base waxes (sometimes called sealer-waxes), and running waxes (sometimes called kicking, climbing or glide waxes). Running waxes are broadly broken down into hard waxes, and 'klisters'. A first point is that the colder and newer the snow, the harder the wax. Klisters are for old, soft snow, and in "above zero" temperatures.

BASIC WAXING RULES

If you follow the following rules most of your problems will be little ones.

1. Stick to one manufacturer's brand of wax.
2. Read the instructions on can or tube before applying.
3. Remember a soft wax gives more grip than a hard wax, but less glide.
4. Remember that you can put a soft wax on a hard wax but not vice-versa.
5. Wax neatly, making a good job improves the result.
6. Several *thin* layers give more grip than one *thick* one.

7. If you have too much 'grip' try rubbing the wax out thinner with a cork.
8. Remember that freezing point is 0°C or 32°F. Above 0°C the snow is wet — below 0°C the snow is dry.
9. Learn to judge the snow by feel (Page 35).
10. Apply the wax to dry skis — it won't go on otherwise.

Now, since that seems a lot of rules, let's just go into the reasoning.

1. Most manufacturers code waxes by colour, but use a different range of colours. Stick to one brand and you'll know where you are.
2. For the same reason read the instructions, one man's 'klister' is another man's poison! Waxes come in cans, klister in tubes.
3. & 4. If you put a hard wax on top of a soft wax it will just cut through — because it's harder! You will have to scrape the soft wax off to apply a hard wax — so if in doubt use a harder wax first.
5, 6 & 7. A neat job gives better results. Read the application instructions and 'cork' the job properly if required. A good corking improves a good waxing, and you can often thin out the wax by rubbing it down with a cork and get more glide, without scraping the lot off and starting again.
8 & 9. The basic decision is between wet and dry snow, but the permutations are endless. See waxing chart (page 35).
10. That's why we told you to buy a ski bag for transportation. You are better off waxing indoors, but the skis must be put outside to adjust to the temperature before you start to ski.

WAXING KIT

The basic kit consists of just three items:

1. Some waxes and klisters (Page 32).
2. A waxing cork.
3. A scraper.

Buy a plastic bag to put them in, as loose waxes can make a mess. As time goes on and you get more experienced you will also want:—

4. Solvents (for cleaning the wax off).
5. A waxing iron — for melting and spreading wax on skis.
6. A waxing torch; a mini-blowtorch for putting on base wax, removing old wax, and warming the waxing iron.

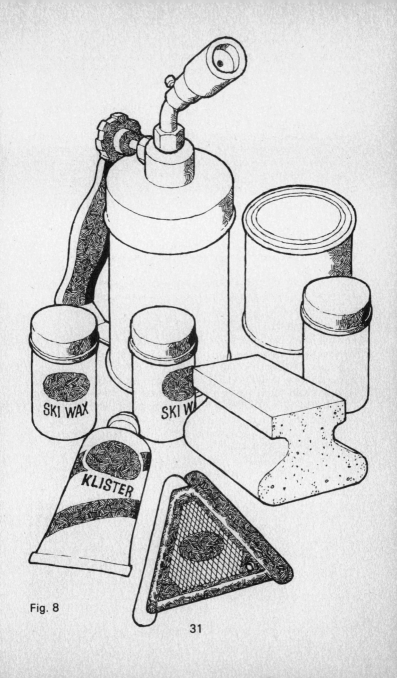

Fig. 8

WAXES AND KLISTERS

Each major manufacturer supplies about a dozen running waxes and klisters, plus a range of base preparations, compounds and cleaners.

'Running waxes' fall into two groups:

Hard Waxes: These come in little colour coded cans, and are, broadly speaking used for new dry snow, and powder.

Klisters: 'Klister' is a Norwegian word, meaning 'sticky', and klisters are sticky waxes that come in colour-coded tubes or sometimes in aerosol cans. Klister is used for older, slushy, or settled packed snow. It gives grip.

To this basic range we have to add:

Glide Waxes: These are often paraffin based, and go on plastic or fibreglass bottoms — even on the tips and tails of non-wax skis — to increase *glide.*

Base Waxes (sealers): These are used to help running waxes adhere to the ski, and are used on synthetic skis and the wood-soled variety.

Base Preparations (Tars): These are not waxes at all. Tars are used to seal wooden skis against damp, and provide a base for the base waxes.

HOW TO WAX

If you have wooden skis, you will need to apply a tar base. This is then covered with a base wax. From this point on the waxing drill is basically the same for all sorts of ski surfaces.

1. Check the snow. The type of wax and the method of application depends on the snow state. Is it new or old, hard crust or powder, above or below freezing? The glove test (Page 35) is a good simple guide.

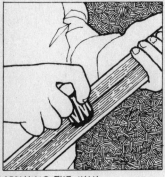
APPLYING THE WAX.
Fig. 9

SMOOTHING WAX WITH A CORK.

2. Select a wax, and READ THE INSTRUCTIONS on tube or can.
3. Wax indoors if possible, and be sure the skis are clean, dry and free from grit and old wax.
4. Apply the wax, covering the entire surface of the ski. The higher the temperature, the rougher the surface of the wax finish should be, so apply the wax roughly.
5. If you need good glide, cork the wax out smoothly.
6. Put the skis outside to adjust to the cold, and then *test your wax* by ski-ing around for a few minutes. If you have too much grip, cork the wax out some more. If not enough grip, put on some more wax, in a rough surface.

KLISTERS

Klisters come in tubes, and to apply them successfully you need to warm up the tubes first, and then apply the klister indoors. Smooth out the klister with the heel of the hand. It's messy, but you can wipe your hands clean in the snow.

Put on a thin layer first, as removing klister is a difficult operation. You will also need some warmth to get the stuff off.

BASE WAXES

Synthetic skis don't hold running waxes as well as wood, and you will need to apply a base wax to the synthetic to provide a binder for the running wax. You can get spray-on base wax preparations, or you can paint or melt base-wax on from a can.

REMOVING THE WAX

The three common methods of removing waxes are:
1. By scraper.
2. By melting it off with a blowtorch.
3. By the use of solvents.

A scraper is a basic item, and which of the other two you use, depends on their availability. Don't spray solvents onto the ski. It is better to damp a soft rag and wipe it over the wax in order to remove it.

WAXING AREAS

Because I believe it is better, I recommend that you wax the whole ski. Many authorities recommend that you need only wax the "kicking" area — that is the area under the foot, and indeed some synthetic skis have a marked scale in this waxing area to

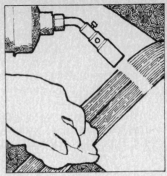

SCRAPING OFF OLD WAX.   REMOVING WAX WITH BLOWTORCH

Fig. 10

help you remember how much of it you have covered. Others recommend a 'kicking' wax in this area, and 'glide' waxes on tip and tail. Many experienced ski tourers recommend using a paraffin glide wax in the ski groove, which collects ice, rather than a running wax. The permutations are endless, and the aim is the same — to ski cross-country with ease. Experience will teach you which method works best for you — so don't worry.

However, the beginner can avoid much of this waxing toil and expense if, initially anyway, he sticks to using Universal, or 'Wide-Range' waxes.

WIDE RANGE WAXES

The basic idea of a wide range wax is that it cuts the waxing decisions down to one. Is it above or below freezing? Put another way, is the snow wet — (above 0°C) or dry — (below 0°C).

Wide range waxes reduce the calculations still further by naming the waxes in a simple fashion. Most major manufacturers have a wide range wax, for example:

SNOW	TEMP	MANUFACTURER		
		REX	SWIX	TOKO
Wet	Above 0°C	Plus	Plus	Plus
Dry	Below 0°C	Minus	Minus	Minus

It could hardly be easier!

34

CHECKING THE SNOW

Most cross country ski-ers prefer to check the temperature by the state of the snow, rather than by using a thermometer, which just records the air temperature. Cross-country ski-ers use the 'glove test'.

You pick up a handful of snow in your gloved hand and squeeze it. Open your hand and see what's happened.

1. A snowball has formed, or moisture on the glove = WET SNOW.
2. If the snow blows away = DRY SNOW.

It may sound crude, but for the touring ski-er it's quite adequate. Now all you have to do is select a wax, and put it on the ski. (See charts below).

If it has snowed overnight, or it is still falling, use this chart:—

FALLING OR NEW SNOW

SNOW STATE	MANUFACTURER			
	TOKO	SWIX	REX	RODE
Fine flakes	Olive or green	Green	Green	Green
Dry flakes	Blue	Blue	Blue	Blue
Forms a snowball (moist)	Red	Violet or Yellow	Violet or Yellow	Violet or Yellow
Leaves hand wet (wet)	Yellow or Red Klister	Yellow Klister	Red Klister	Red Klister

If the snow is a day or two old it has settled, so use this chart:

SETTLED SNOW

SNOW STATE	MANUFACTURER			
	TOKO	SWIX	REX	RODE
Small grains	Green	Green	Green	Green
Large grains, lumps	Blue or Violet	Blue	Blue or Violet Klister	Blue
Forms wet snowball	Yellow	Blue or Violet	Red or Red Klister	Violet
Leaves hands very wet.	Red or Violet Klister	Red Klister	Red Klister	Red or Silver Klister

After a few days, with warm days and freezing nights, the snows construction starts to break down; it has *metamorphised,* so you use this one:

OLD (METAMORPHISED) SNOW

SNOW STATE	MANUFACTURER			
	TOKO	SWIX	REX	RODE
Hard crust 'skare'	Blue Klister	Blue Klister	Blue	Red Klister
Crumbly granulated	Violet Klister	Violet Klister	Violet Klister	Blue or Violet Klister
Melting wet	Red Klister	Red Klister	Silver or Red Klister	Silver or black Klister

Please note that these charts leave out the many variations: Light Greens — Special Blues etc., — also that where two colours appear in one box the second one is the one to use when the snow may be wetter, or melting.

FIBREGLASS SKIS

For recreational or touring ski-ers, the whole ski should be waxed. Make a special job of the camber area under the foot for this is where the 'kick' takes effect. It does not matter in which direction you spread the wax, but remember that the wider you spread the wax, whatever its colour, the more grip you get. This may not be a snag, for you may *want* more grip with that wax. On the other hand the more you polish it on or cork it out, the more glide you get.

NON-WAX SKIS

I find it necessary to put a paraffin "glide"-wax on my non-wax skis. Applied thinly, it helps on the flat and downhill, while otherwise the skis seem a little slow. I put this on the tail of the ski, behind the 'cut', and well forward on the "shovel" leaving a good gap so that it cannot work back into the 'cut'-section.

WOODEN SKIS

Unless covered with a plastic or fibreglass coat, the base of the wood ski will have to be treated with tar to exclude the wet and damp. You can buy tars which you put on with a spray or brush, or tars which have to be melted (not burned) on to the wood ski base. Depending upon the amount of use you give them, wooden sole skis may need tarring once or twice a season.

The tar must be covered with a full length covering of base wax, and this is, in turn, followed by the running waxes.

RUNNING IN

No wax will perform efficiently until it has been used for a little while. Don't expect much until you have covered say a quarter of a mile on skis, (.3 km.).

ADVICE

The best piece of advice I have had on waxing was to use my eyes and if in doubt, ask. If you see someone motoring along, better than the rest, with great ease, ask him how he is waxed. Store up such advice for future use and don't be too embarrassed to ask for it.

Chapter 6

TECHNIQUE
MOVING, TURNING, STOPPING

The basic movement of cross country is the diagonal stride, or 'pas alternatif', as the French call it. Essentially it is a loping striding slide, the arms swinging forward, shoulders high and back, giving impetus to the stride.

Many experts define the diagonal stride as an extension of the normal walking movement, but it isn't as simple as that. To learn the knack I suggest you try out the following.

DIAGONAL STRIDE

Find a flat piece of snow, up to 50 metres long, and position yourself at one end, skis parallel and about 6" (15 cm.) apart. Now start to walk across the snow, left leg first, swinging the right arm shoulder high, lifting and placing the right pole just forward of the right boot, the pole slanting back from the wrist.

Continue, swing the arms alternately, left leg,-right arm, right arm-left leg. Make a positive movement, and avoid weak swings which will end up with you swinging the right arm with the right leg!

After about six or seven paces when the arms are going well, lean forward, bend the knees and *kick* with the rear foot, sliding the first foot forward. This is a powerful skating movement, and you must take advantage of it, to prolong the glide as far as possible.

As you slide, bring the rear foot up with alternate arm, plant pole, kick, slide, alternate arm swing, plant pole, kick!—and you're off. **Two points:** Keep the arms swinging and the *knees bent.* You can't kick with a straight leg. And keep going, don't stop kicking.' **Two .more points:** Don't plod. You can kick and slide quite slowly, but keep the movement going.

Fig. 11

You may find it easier to begin with if you practise without poles. They help balance and provide push, but they are something extra to think about. Try a few circuits without poles first, to get the arms swinging properly.

The diagonal stride is not dissimilar to a skating movement, but fore and aft. Once you get the idea — which should be the first time, if you follow these instructions, you will start to cover the ground quickly and easily, with firm kicks and long glides. But don't just kick and slide forward in the same position. Having kicked, the rear foot should be unweighted and coming through to glide, while the *other* leg kicks. Don't let the first kicking leg trail.

POLE TECHNIQUE

Examine the diagram (Fig. 12) carefully. Note that the pole *slants to the rear.* Don't stab forward, as if to gain ground. The pole provides about twenty-five percent of your impetus if it is applied to the REAR, so don't waste the movement. Remember also to keep the arms at shoulder height apart, swinging them close to the sides. Don't spread them wide as this again wastes effort.

If you grip the poles tightly and heave yourself forward by the arms you will tire yourself out very quickly. Grasp the poles lightly, bearing down on the strap, and letting the grip slacken until, as you near the end of the movement, the pole is grasped between thumb and first finger, ready to swing forward.

Fig. 12

Fig. 13

DOUBLE POLING

You can use this to gain speed while sliding or for extra impetus when doing the diagonal stride.

Swing both arms forward together, placing the poles firmly and swinging through to the rear. It's pretty tiring, but it can be useful when striding. Save effort by taking two kick and glide strides between each pole thrust. Use the weight of the body not the strength of your arms to power the poles back. (Fig. 13)

TURNING

Stopped on the flat, you can just shuffle round, taking care not to let the tails or tips cross. It's not very graceful but it gets you there. On a slope you use the kick turn, which is also useful, as illustrated here (Fig. 14) for crossing obstacles.

KICK TURNS

The secret of a successful kick turn is to plant the poles clear of the skis. The most simple rule is *'Plant the pole to the rear of the first ski you move.'* This will cover you for all eventualities, for you swing your ski round the planted pole, transfer the weight, and bring the other ski over.

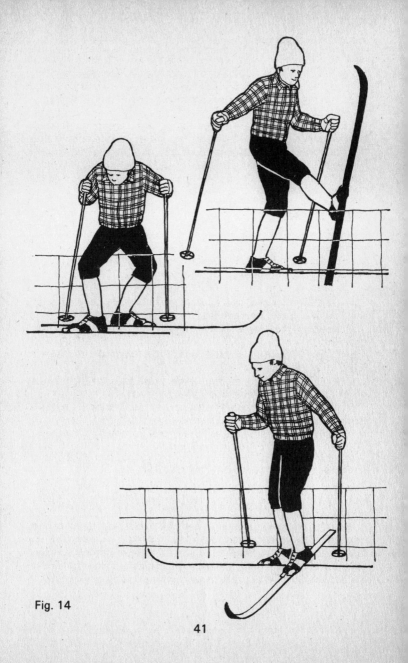

Fig. 14

41

SKATING TURNS

Next to the diagonal stride the skate turn is the most useful technique, and one you will need all the time. A neat skate turn gets you out of rutted tramlines, past a fallen friend, or round a tree. Time spent learning and practising it will not be wasted.

Let us assume a turn to the right. Start double poling and bend the knees. For a skate turn, be sure you are running on parallel skis. Transfer all your weight on the left ski, while you lift the right one which is then pointed off 45° into the new direction. Now kick off the left weighted ski, transferring the weight on to the right gliding one. Bring the left ski parallel and off you go in the new direction. Now try it to the left. (Fig. 15)

STEM TURNS

It's important to remember that most cross-country skis have no metal edges. Therefore turns, especially the stem turn, must be executed by transferring the weight, and not by carving the turns, as you can do with heavy, edged downhill skis.

The stem is used for turning at the end of a traverse.

1. Run the traverse, skis apart, knees bent, weight evenly on the skis; turn point approaches.

2. Keeping the knees bent, transfer *all* the weight to the downhill ski.

3. Stem, by pushing out the rear of the upper ski, to make a wide 'V' of the tips.

4. Keeping the upper ski flat in the snow, transfer the weight on to it. Lean *out* as your body swings round.

5. Once round, the weight is still on the outside (downhill) ski. Bring in the unweighted upper ski, spread the weight evenly and continue the traverse. Repeat the process for the next turn (Fig. 16).

STOPPING: SNOWPLOUGH STOP

You *can,* when you get very good, do jump turns in order to stop. Until then you will rely on the snowplough position to slow down, and stop you.

For this, the knees are bent, and the heels, well down on the heel plate are forced out, the ski tips making a 'V'. Keep the ski tips together and you will soon stop. Cross-country ski-ers are cautious about descending slopes without a good clear run out at the bottom. So now let's talk about climbing up and coming down.

Fig. 15

SKATE TURN

Fig. 16

STEM TURN

Chapter 7

GOING UP AND COMING DOWN

The uninitiated are amazed that the cross-country ski-er can, on the same wax, ski fast down hill, zip along the flat, and climb steep slopes. The secret lies in the waxing, good techniques, and in the effects of friction. When the ski is in motion, friction melts the snow under it, and gives glide. When the ski stops, this melting stops too, and you get adhesion, and adequate grip for kicking or climbing.

CLIMBING

Diagonal Stride: The diagonal stride will get you up most reasonable slopes if you remember to keep the weight forward, and the knees bent.

Don't try for a long glide. Short, even strides will get you there, together with short thrusts from the poles. The crucial thing is to keep the weight forward and move on your toes.

Running Stride: A shorter, but steeper slope can be overcome by taking it at a run. Bound forward, throwing the weight from the rear to front ski, and your impetus will probably get you there. If not, you will have three remaining choices.

(1) Side Stepping: Start at the bottom, skis at right angles to the fall line, weight on lower ski and lift the upper ski to the side. Transfer the weight on to it. Bring up the lower leg. Repeat until you get to the top. (Fig. 17)

It is very important to keep the skis parallel to the fall line, or you can slide away forward or back.

(2) Herringbone: The Herringbone takes its name from the pattern the skis leave behind in fresh snow.

Facing the slope, point the skis out sideways, heels together in the reverse of the snowplough (Fig. 17). Keep the knees bent in together and climb the slope. The herringbone is much faster, but more tiring than the side step, but is useful for short steep slopes.

(3) Traverse Turns: Big wide slopes lend themselves to the traverse turns. Take the slope at an angle, and zig-zagging your way up, use alternative strides, single poled, for the traverse, and an uphill skating, or kick turn for the corners. You will need to edge the skis for the turns, or, if the slope is very steep or icy, use the kick turn across your own uphill tracks. (Fig. 18)

Fig. 17

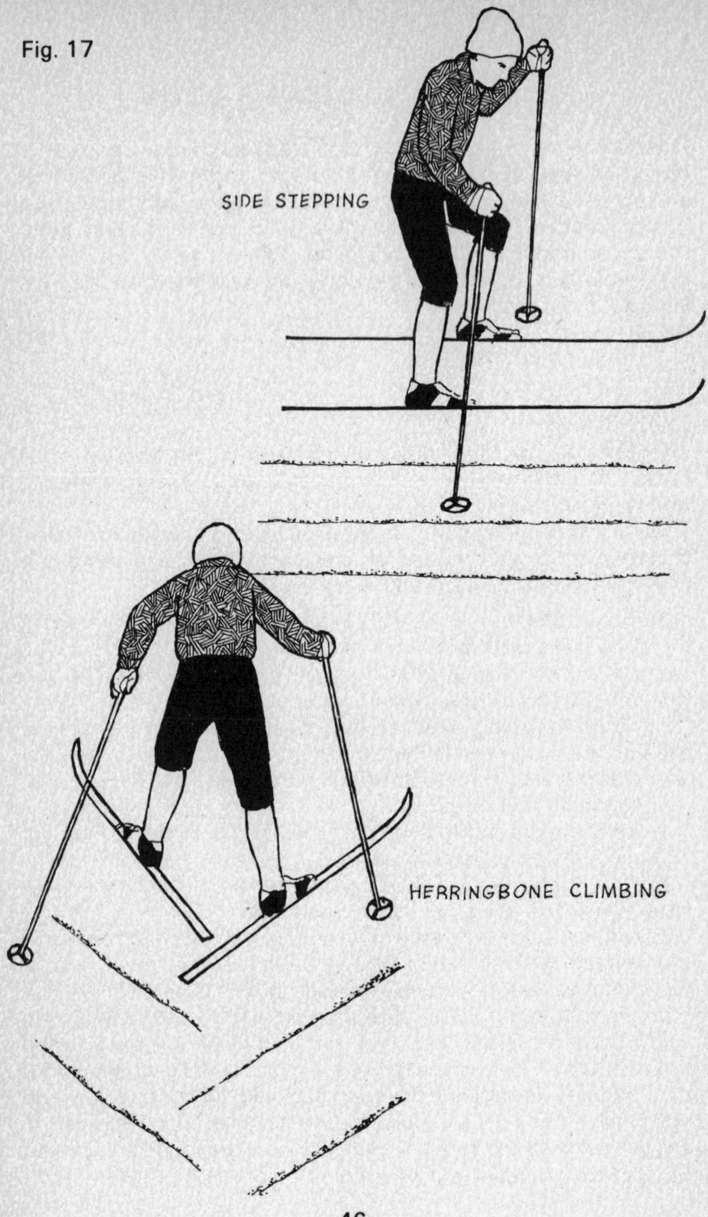

SIDE STEPPING

HERRINGBONE CLIMBING

Fig. 18

COMING DOWN

Schuss: The easiest is the straight, skis parallel, downhill run. Stay upright, weight even on both feet, and let yourself go. Keeping the knees bent and holding the poles out at right angles to the body can help you to maintain balance while crossing bumps.

If your path takes you through trees or bush, remove the hands from the pole loops. If the basket catches on a branch you may drop the pole, but if your hand is in the loop you will get a badly wrenched arm as well.

Traversing: Turning: On a long steep slope, with a cluttered or obscured run out, run down the hill in a zig-zag traverse turning with the skate turn, or stem turn, on even slopes, or using the kick turn if the slope looks too steep.

Telemark Turn: The Telemark turn is a beautiful movement. You have all seen the Telemark position probably on television, for it is the position that ski jumpers adopt on landing. Knees are bent, rear leg trails, arms are held out wide. From this you can gather that the Telemark position looks and feels, very stable. The turn itself needs some two hours hard work on the slope to perfect. (Fig. 19)

Find an even slope, preferably with light snow cover, and go to the top.

1. Start down, with the knees bent, and with the skis slightly ploughed.

2. Slide one ski well ahead of the other, until the **binding** of the forward ski is level with the **tip** of the rear ski. All your weight is forward, the rear ski is trailing.

3. Keep the poles out at right angles to aid stability.

4. Now stem the forward ski slightly and you will go round in a wide graceful turn. If your right leg is in front you stem it out, to turn to the right.

5. Let the rear ski trail and remember that the rear leg is bent, and below the knee is parallel to the trailing ski.

6. Expect a few falls before you get the knack. Learning a Telemark turn is rather like learning to ride a bicycle. Once you get the hang of it you don't fall off so much!

Linked Telemark turns are an excellent way of descending a wide long open slope that is not too steep. You can build up a considerable speed on cross-country skis, **so be careful.**

Fig. 19

TELE MARK TURN

Fig. 20

WALL CROSSING

Chapter 8

OBSTACLE CROSSING

By its very nature cross-country ski-ing takes the ski-er up to obstacles. Since it is not always possible to remove the skis to cross them, the cross-country ski-er has evolved ways of doing so while keeping the skis on. Snow has often drifted deeply against walls and fences, so you must keep your skis on to avoid sinking. Remember that cross country equipment is light, so that given a little agility you will soon be able to perform these manoeuvres without difficulty.

LOW FENCES

Use the kick turn. Stop parallel with the fence, and place one pole over on to the other side, level with the rear of the skis. Now lift the inner ski up, over, round and down. You are now straddling the fence. Bring the other leg over, and away you go. (Fig. 14)

LOW WALLS

Stand parallel with the wall, and if it is snow covered, step up onto it. Now bring up the other leg, then one ski down, then the other. If the drop is greater on the other side, put the poles down and jump off, feet together.

BACK ROLLS

If the wall is wide or up to waist high, try rolling over it on your back. Sit or lean back on the wall. Lie down on the top, lifting the skis, and roll over to put the feet flat on the far side. (Fig. 20)

FENCE JUMP

For obstacles up to elbow height, try jumping. Find a fence post and stand parallel with the fence. Remove the hands from the pole straps and place the poles close to the outer ski. Place the other hand on the fence post, and swing between post and poles. Take a breath and:—

1. Swing up, bending the knees to raise the skis.
2. Jump round, twisting over the fence.
3. Land on both skis on the far side facing the other way.

As with the Telemark, it's a knack, and needs a little practice. Start with waist-high fences if you like. An obstacle crossing 'follow-my-leader' game, played to and fro over a fence, is the best way to get everybody going on this very useful XC skill. (Fig. 21)

Fig. 21

HUP!

52

STREAMS

Be wary of streams. Don't splash across with your skis on, or they will ice up when you reach the snow. Try and find a snow bridge, but only if it is not too wide or the stream not too deep. Use fallen trees, or go higher up until the stream narrows. Use bridges—that's what they are for.

ROADS

Don't forget to check if anything is coming. Step on to the road, and lift the feet high when crossing. Do not slither or you will scrape the wax off, or damage the surface of your non-wax ski.

Chapter 9

DAY TOURING

Let us assume that you have started your cross-country ski-ing, with a week's holiday. After three days instruction you should be ready to undertake a little tour. You won't be very expert, but you can get along, and one way to improve skill and build up stamina is to go for a day tour.

EQUIPMENT

There must be at least three in the party. You need to carry, apart from normal clothes, skis and poles, a rucksack with the following items:—

1. Spare warm clothing.
2. Compass and map; (can you use them?)
3. Extra ski tip.
4. First aid kit.
5. Warm food in vacuum flask and/or
6. Food plus stove.
7. Whistle.
8. 'Space' blanket.
9. Matches.
10. Candles.

Take this, even for a half-day's outing. If you are going all day then you should also take:

11. Sleeping bags.
12. Light tent.

You may get stuck out overnight. Someone may get a touch of exposure. These items add little to your load—and in return take a bigger load off your mind.

However, if you are going on a short tour, on well marked and frequented trails, you may well decide to carry less. It is, however, as well to be prepared, and get in the **habit** of safety. This equipment spread among three or more people will hardly be noticed.

ROUTES

Work out your routes beforehand, and prepare a route card. This simply notes the compass bearings and map references for each part of the trip, and puts in the timings. On skis your speed over similar distances can vary immensely from a few hundred yards in an hour to a speed of 20 mph or more. It depends on the terrain. Study the contours on the map and make calculated time estimates, noting these down on the route card.

Next, have your calculations checked, so that any error is noticed.

SAFETY

Leave a copy of the route card behind, or placed somewhere visible in your car. If your party fails to return, someone will at least have an idea of where you might be.

DAYLIGHT TIME

Remember that in winter, daylight hours are short, and often made even shorter in mountain country by changing weather or low cloud.

DISTANCES

Cross-country ski-ing can be tiring work, so don't attempt too much to begin with. Remember that 10 km. out means another 10 km back, and that's 20 kms. Always choose a terrain and distance that is well within the capacity of the weakest member of the party. I recommend that you go no more than 8 km. (5 miles) out and back, until you are fitter, and confident in the snow.

WAXES

It is quite likely that during the day, and by covering a distance, you will meet changing or totally different snow conditions. Take some spare waxes and a scraper.

Chapter 10

SNOW AND WINTER HAZARDS

The cross-country ski-er has to be far more concerned with the state of the snow than does the downhill ski-er. The downhill ski-er usually skis on prepared 'piste,' regularly serviced by snow-cats or amtracks, and his heavier steel edged skis ride over or through ruts and ice which could disconcert the cross-country ski-er with his lighter equipment, who usually travels off-piste anyway.

Many places do, in fact, have prepared touring trails for the cross-country ski-er, over the hills and through the woods. Some even get provided with 'tramlines' to take the skis, but even here, because of the variation in terrain, and the presence of trees, the snow surface can change and this of course, affects the waxing. Finally, an understanding of snow is a useful aid when it comes to waxing itself.

FALLING SNOW

Snowflakes are composed of crystals. One estimate has it that there are some 6000 different kinds of snowflake. Temperature decides the form they take while falling, and if it is warm, the crystals can jam up into large wet flakes, or if it is very cold, you can get the little soft pellets, or 'granules,' which are caused by the flakes falling through fog or cloud.

The state of falling snow can change even as it falls and wet (over 0°C) and dry (under 0°C) snow, can be contained in the same snowfall.

NEW SNOW

Broadly speaking, snow is defined as 'wet' or 'dry' and can vary from 'very dry' which is very light and can be kicked up or swirled about like dust, to a heavy, clinging type, that soaks through your clothes, and will form a snowball if squeezed in the hand.

METAMORPHISM

As soon as a snowflake hits the earth, it starts to change, and this change is one of a series, collectively referred to as *Metamorphism*. The first noticeable effect of this is that a fall of fresh snow, high and fluffy, will settle into a more even and cohesive mass within a few days. This is caused by the melting and fusing together of the original snow crystals. Powder snow develops up to three days *after a fall*.

As snow fall follows snow fall, each fall has different characteristics, and the temperature within each layer can vary. The lower layers, under pressure from above, are continually melting, and water vapour from below is extracted into the upper layer. The lower crystals are continually growing together, and changing shape, and this process is referred to scientifically as *constructive metamorphism*. They eventually form what are known as cup-crystals, which are quite large, up to half an inch long, and, naturally, cup-shaped.

This is a sketchy outline, but you can see a pattern of light, insignificant snow on the top, increasing as you go down to larger ice crystals at the bottom. These varying shapes are continually changing, but do not mix. It is as if fine sand was layered on top of gravel, which in turn rested on large pebbles.

The next stage, often found in early spring, is produced by the continual melting and refreezing of surface snow, which produces a coarse snow, often encountered on the sunny side of mountains.

WIND AND SNOW

The wind blows the snow about, forming drifts, and also shapes the heavier snow, forming ridges and cornices on the edges of escarpments. The wind pressure and the movement thus created can melt the crystals, and they then refreeze into hard wind-slabs, and stepped snow faces. Drift snow in the lee of trees or rocks can be of quite different composition from the snow all about it, and is often deep and soft.

SKARE

Hard, icy snow, rutted and wind driven, is often referred to as 'skare'. It is hard stuff to ski on, and calls for careful waxing.

A knowledge of snow, is the basis of snow craft, one of the fundamental skis needed by cross country ski-ers, and ski-mountaineers. Snow, apart from being our highway, and travel surface, is also our greatest hazard. The mountains, in winter, need to be treated with respect, and a knowledge of possible hazards will go a long way towards avoiding them.

"It's perfectly safe, as long as you remember it's dangerous."

A demolition instructor coined that useful phrase, when referring to plastic explosive, but it's a remark well worth remembering in connection with outdoor activities in winter.

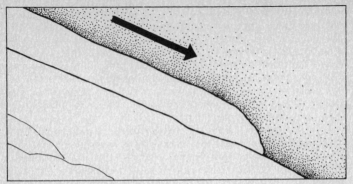

FLOWING AVALANCHE

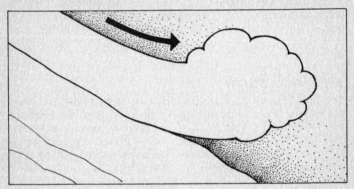

AIRBORNE POWDER AVALANCHE

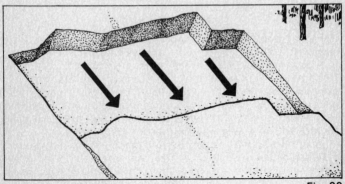

SLAB AVALANCHE

Fig. 22

AVALANCHES (FIG. 22)

Most of the people killed or maimed by avalanches are ski-ers. Downhill ski-ers have some protection as they operate on prepared runs, under the watchful eye of local people and safety teams, who not only mark out safe runs, but remove impending dangers, often dislodging possible avalanches with dynamite. The best way to remove an avalanche is to create one, and the 'boom' of explosions doing just that, is a common sound in the mountains in winter.

CARELESSNESS AND STUPIDITY

Most of the people killed every year are killed by carelessness. They ignore warning signs, ski round barriers, and run across avalanche slopes, often refusing to halt when ordered to. Even worse, sometimes the first ski-ers get away with it and their tracks, curving across that inviting slope, lure others out to their deaths.

NEVER:
1. Ignore avalanche warnings.
2. Ski past barriers, or on closed routes.
3. Ignore the advice of instructors, guides or avalanche teams.

Stress the danger to less experienced friends. Avalanches — make no mistake about it — are killers.

TYPES OF AVALANCHE

Avalanches can occur almost anywhere. Tree-covered slopes, with a gradient of less than 15° can avalanche. People have been killed by avalanches less than 20 metres wide, flowing only a hundred yards. The snow collapsed under them, swallowed them up, settled over them and the pressure forced it to freeze, burying them alive.

LOOSE SNOW AVALANCHES

After a fall of new snow, it can, as it settles, slip from the old base snow, and avalanche. Provided the rate of slide is slow, loose snow avalanches are not too dangerous, but if the slope is long and the speed builds up it can develop into the next, and very lethal, variety.

AIRBORNE-POWDER AVALANCHE

In these, the snow gains momentum, flies into the air, and creates a terrific blast and suction. They travel at great speed, up to 200 mph and are amazingly destructive, shattering buildings, stripping trees from a slope, hurling buses and cars from roads. They are not unlike localized hurricanes. One such avalanche struck a busload of ski-ers in Switzerland and killed 24 out of the 35 on board.

WET SNOW AVALANCHES

These are most common in the spring, when the snow melts. They tend to be slow, but heavy, and ski-ers caught in them will be crushed to death, but luckily they are slow, often follow regular routes, and occur at a predictable time of the year.

SLAB AVALANCHES

These happen when a complete slab of snow breaks away in a unit, and plunges into the valley. They often occur on open grass slopes, and can come from snow packed into slabs by wind action.

Slab snow is always dangerous because the wind action has formed it into a mass, without having blended it to the surface beneath. It is therefore hanging up there by its own weight, and even the slightest pressure or movement can loosen it. Ski-ers are at particular risk from this sort of avalanche, for the snow looks so even and attractive that they are tempted on to it.

Stay off slab snow on open slopes.

AVALANCHE PRECAUTIONS

The best precaution is to use common sense, listen to advice, and obey any signs or warnings.

Cross-country ski-ers, whose favoured terrain is country where avalanches occur, should travel in parties, and only cross slopes singly, having deployed an *oertal* cord behind them. An *oertal* cord is a length or red line, which you trail behind you. If you go under there is a good chance that this line will still be visible on the surface, and you can be located before you suffocate.

Before you cross a dodgy slope, try and test it first, by shouting, or throwing stones or snowballs out onto the snow. If nothing happens, loosen the ski bindings, remove the hands from the pole loops, and cross singly. Rope up the leader if possible.

If the slope carries someone away, watch where he disappears. If you feel the slope going get rid of skis and poles, for the snow wrenching them can fracture your arms and legs. Try 'swimming' to stay near the surface. Keep the mouth shut and as

60

the slide slows, try and clear a space around the mouth and chest to give you breathing room.

Those on the surface should search the slope, and try and locate the victim first, before sending for an avalanche team. Speed is essential in avalanche rescue.

There is a lot more to avalanches and this outline is only designed to acquaint you with the danger, and probability. Perhaps this knowledge will come in useful one day. To learn more, I would recommend that you read Colin Fraser's excellent and readable 'Avalanche Enigma' (John Murray 1966), or if you prefer a fictional, but factually correct thriller, read Desmond Bagley's, 'The Snow Tiger' (Fontana 1976).

WIND CHILL

The hills are windy, and cross-country ski-ing is warm work. This can lead to the ski-er taking inadequate precautions against the elements, which may be fine when you are moving, but is not to be recommended when you stop. In particular, beware of the wind-chill factor. The theory of wind-chill is founded on the fact that once the temperature gets below $0°C$, any wind will intensify the effect of the cold, in direct ratio to its strengh. Observe the following chart.

WIND CHILL CHART

Wind Speed	Local Temperature (F)			
0	32	23	14	5
5	29	20	10	1
10	18	7	−4	−15
15	13	−1	−13	−25
20	7	−6	−19	−32
30	1	−13	−27	−41

Note then, and don't forget, that the *effective* temperature can, thanks to the wind, be much lower than the true air temperature, and this can lead to such irritations as chapped skin, cracked lips, frost nip, and even more serious, frost-bite.

FROST BITE

If you perspire, your undergarments and sweaters can get wet. Wet clothing, however it gets wet, loses its insulation.

Wet socks or sweat-soaked shirts are no protection, so change the first and cover up the second.

True frost-bite is not very common, but frost nip or the cracking of skin exposed to severe cold is quite prevelent. A good lip-salve or a barrier cream can help a lot.

To prevent frost-bite, maintain body warmth and avoid tight laces and constricting clothing. Stay dry. Wear wool, avoid synthetics, and keep the extremities, feet, toes, fingers, nose and ears, protected and warm.

TREATMENT

The frosted part will go white and feel dead. Warm the affected part slowly, with body warmth. Fingers can be held in the mouth or under the armpit, toes can be held under a friend's sweater. Never rub the affected part directly, least of all with snow.

Restore warmth slowly. If a warm bath is available start with tepid water and warm it gradually. Never rush the re-warming process.

As with avalanches, be aware of the danger. Frost-bite may be rare, but the effects are unpleasant.

EXPOSURE (Hypothermia)

The condition referred to as 'exposure' is caused by inadequate protection against cold, wet and wind. On their own, neither of these three need bother the ski-er. In combination they can be lethal. Hypothermia, which can be the end result of exposure, is severe loss of body heat, and can cause death.

Prevention is the best answer. Correct clothing, regular food, and adequate rest, will avoid exposure. The symptoms of exposure come on slowly at first, then with increasing severity and rapidity. Uncharacteristic stumbling, speaking in a slurred voice, becoming withdrawn, stupidity, or sometimes sudden bursts of chatter, listlessness, may be signs of exposure — don't shrug them off. Once the victim collapses you have a severe problem.

TREATMENT

STOP and get out of the wind. If the victim is in the early stages and conscious, get him or her warm. Make a shelter or form a windbreak. Dry the casualty and get him into dry clothes. Cover up the head and hands — thirty per cent of the body's heat loss is from the head — give him a hot drink from the vacuum flask. If possible get him into a space blanket or sleeping bag. However, if

Fig. 23

THE RECOVERY POSITION

you are on a day tour you probably won't have one, but a large plastic bag is an excellent substitute, particularly if it's large enough for someone else to get in beside the victim, to create extra warmth.

If the victim is unconscious, then the situation is very serious and medical aid should be obtained as quickly as possible. Do not force any drinks into an unconscious person. Place the victim in the Recovery Position (Fig. 23). The basic rule in cases of exposure is to re-warm the victim as fast as is reasonably possible, while cutting out the elements which caused the condition to arise. So, shelter, rest and warmth are the answers.

GETTING LOST

Never go into the hills or mountains in winter on your own. There should be at least three people in the party, you should carry overnight gear — just in case, and leave a note of your intended route behind.

Every member should have a local map and compass and know how to use it.

A full range of information on this subject can be found in other Venture Guides, and a list of other titles can be found in the beginning of this book. If you are sensible, and have a sound grasp of outdoor skills, you will find in cross-country ski-ing the activity for a lifetime.